# Extraterrestrial Deception

"Even makes fire come down from heaven."
Revelation 13:13

*Exposing
the Second
Beast's Identity
and its
Source of Power*

Charles Pretlow

**Extraterrestrial Deception**
*Exposing the Second Beast's Identity and its Source of Power*
May 2021

Copyright © Charles Pretlow, printed in the United States of America. No part of this message can be copied or reproduced without written permission by Wilderness Voice Publishing and the author.

Unless otherwise indicated, all Scripture quotations are from the Holy Bible, English Standard Version ® (ESV®), copyright © 2001 by Crossway, a publishing ministry of Good Publishers. Used by permission. All rights reserved.

Portions of some Scripture passages may be underlined at the author's discretion to highlight their importance for clarity and illumination.

ISBN 978-1-943412-11-2

Published by
Wilderness Voice Publishing
PO Box 857
Canon City, CO 81215

"A voice crying in the wilderness –
proclaiming the good news of the coming Kingdom!"

# Contents

| | |
|---|---|
| Introduction | 4 |
| The Deceiver of the Whole World | 7 |
| Powers of Darkness Removing Obstacles | 8 |
| The Wicked Given Over to a Delusion | 9 |
| Also, Wholesale Christian Deception | 10 |
| Prosperity and the Love of This Age | 11 |
| Asleep at the Darkest Hour | 12 |
| The Mystery of Lawlessness | 13 |
| Political and Spiritual Leadership Vacuum | 13 |
| The Devil Knows His Time Is Short | 14 |
| Setting Up for the Antichrist Rule | 15 |
| The Man of Lawlessness Will Captivate the Masses | 15 |
| Was God an Astronaut? | 16 |
| A Neurotic Obsession With E.T. Beings | 17 |
| Supernatural Powers, Sorcery — Saturating America | 20 |
| Signs and Wonders Syndrome | 23 |
| Christians Duped by the ET Myth | 23 |
| A Fallen Angel Emerges From the Nether Gloom | 26 |
| Does Scripture Clarify the Existence Ancient of Aliens? | 27 |
| Fallen Angels and Demons Lose Invisibility | 28 |
| Conspiracy Theory or Bible Prophesy Unfolding | 28 |
| Signs, Fire, Fear—Forcing Antichrist Worship | 30 |
| Ending Lawlessness, Restoring Control and Order | 31 |
| And Now, America is Morphing Into a Socialistic Hybrid | 33 |
| The Antichrist, a God Chosen by the Gods | 34 |
| True Christianity and Israel in the Way | 35 |
| Sci-Fi Becomes Reality | 37 |
| Utopia: The Cloud, 666 Science, and Fear of Death | 38 |
| The Great Tribulation and the Final Harvests | 39 |
| After the Rapture, God's Wrath and Christ's Return | 41 |
| Knowing the Truth Does Not Make One Ready! | 43 |
| | |
| Contact Information | 45 |
| More About the Author | 45 |

## Introduction

*"Then I saw another beast rising out of the earth. It had two horns like a lamb and it spoke like a dragon. It exercises all the authority of the first beast in its presence, and makes the earth and its inhabitants worship the first beast, whose mortal wound was healed. It performs great signs, even making fire come down from heaven to earth in front of people, and by the signs that it is allowed to work in the presence of the beast it deceives those who dwell on earth, telling them to make an image for the beast that was wounded by the sword and yet lived. And it was allowed to give breath to the image of the beast, so that the image of the beast might even speak and might cause those who would not worship the image of the beast to be slain. Also it causes all, both small and great, both rich and poor, both free and slave, to be marked on the right hand or the forehead, so that no one can buy or sell unless he has the mark, that is, the name of the beast or the number of its name. This calls for wisdom: let the one who has understanding calculate the number of the beast, for it is the number of a man, and his number is 666"*

Revelation 13:11-18

Over the centuries and especially over the last 75 years many have researched, pondered, speculated, guessed, and written about who the antichrist might be, where he originates, and how he comes into power.

The Apostle John, in his vision of the end-times as recorded in Revelation, describes the antichrist as a beast rising from the sea. This is the first of two beasts that John saw in his end-time vision.

We know from Scripture that the first beast is the antichrist. The Bible describes him as the man of lawlessness and the son of destruction who comes into worldwide recognition when chaos and lawlessness become widespread.

The antichrist will declare himself to be God before the world, taking the seat as God in the Jewish Third Temple[1]. Christ called this act of the antichrist the: *"Abomination of desolation spoken of by the prophet Daniel, standing in the holy place"* (Matthew 24:15).

Interestingly, the antichrist declares himself to be God, but is only exercising Satan's (the dragon) power and authority. *"The whole earth marveled as they followed the beast. And they worshiped the dragon, for he had given his authority to the beast, and they worshiped the beast, saying, "Who is like the beast, and who can fight against it?"* (Revelation 13:3-4).

Also, in John's vision there is a second beast rising from the earth. This beast has all the powers of the antichrist (the first beast) and demonstrates those powers to make *"the earth and its inhabitants worship the first beast, whose mortal wound was healed"* (Revelation 13:12).

What is more terrifying, this second beast: *"Performs great signs, even making fire come down from heaven to earth in front of people, and by the signs that it is allowed to work in the presence of the beast it deceives those who dwell on earth, telling them to make an image for the beast that was wounded by the sword and yet lived"* (Revelation 13:13-14).

We know the first beast is a human, and that the second beast speaks like a dragon (satanic-like in nature). Scripture does not inform us where the second beast comes from or if it is human. However, it is satanic in nature.

John also saw in his vision how the antichrist, Satan, and the second beast projected demonic spirits that performed signs to enlist all the leaders of the world to prepare to do battle against God's last days army. In this portion of Revelation, the Apostle John describes the second beast as a false prophet: *"And I saw, coming out of the mouth of the dragon and out of the mouth of the*

---

[1] **The Third Jewish Temple:** The second Jewish temple was destroyed by the Romans just as Jesus predicted. All that is left of the Jewish Temple is a wall by the old Temple Mount. A third Temple is in the prefabricated planning stage, to be built upon the old Temple Mount. In 2018 a reenactment of the first sacrifice in more then 2,000 years took place at the old Temple Mound, on the already prefabricated altar made to exact Biblical specifications.

*beast and out of the mouth of the false prophet, three unclean spirits like frogs. For they are demonic spirits, performing signs, who go abroad to the kings of the whole world, to assemble them for battle on the great day of God the Almighty.* (Revelation 16:13-14).

Why does Satan employ the second beast to boaster the antichrist's new world order? How does the second beast cause fire to come down to earth in front people? What kind of science is used by the second beast to deceive the masses into taking its mark, (666)?

Most important, what kind of being does the second beast appear as, in that the whole world gives heed, causing the people of earth to fall in line and worship the antichrist?

These questions and more will be addressed in this short exposé of Satan's end-time scheme to convince the world to follow and worship the antichrist.

We will uncover how Satan has progressively programmed the masses and many Christians to accept the second beast as a powerful being that knows all, a creature to be feared, and a stern enforcer of the antichrist's new world order.

## The Deceiver of the Whole World

Scripture makes it clear, the god of this world is Satan, at least temporarily. Christ declared the devil to be the ruler of this world as recorded in the Gospel of John.

The Apostle Paul writes that: *"The god of this world has blinded the minds of the unbelievers, to keep them from seeing the light of the gospel of the glory of Christ, who is the image of God"* (2 Corinthians 4:4).

In Revelation the Apostle John speaks of Satan as being like a great fierce dragon and the deceiver of the whole world. (See Revelation 12:9.)

Also, in Apostle John's end-of-this-age vision, two beasts emerge to deceive and gain control of all the peoples of the world. These two beings are Satan's henchmen and are part of the devil's plan to rule all of mankind and attack Christians. *"Also it was allowed to make war on the saints and to conquer them. And authority was given it over every tribe and people and language and nation"* (Revelation 13:7).

The first beast who rises from the sea is referred to in Scripture as a man, *the man of lawlessness*, that is, the antichrist.

However, the second beast in Revelation emerges from the bowels of the Earth which means it is most likely from hell as one of Satan's fallen angels, for it speaks like a dragon (satanic in nature).

*"Then I saw another beast rising out of the earth. It had two horns like a lamb and it spoke like a dragon. It exercises all the authority of the first beast in its presence, and makes the earth and its inhabitants worship the first beast, whose mortal wound was healed. It performs great signs, even making fire come down from heaven to earth in front of people, and by the signs that it is allowed to work in the presence of the beast <u>it deceives those who dwell on earth, telling them to make an image for the beast that was wounded by the sword and yet lived</u>"* (Revelation 13:11-14).

Thus, the first beast (the antichrist), in his efforts to control the whole world receives credibility and backing from the second beast. This is accomplished by the second beast performing great signs and terrifying the world, demanding that the antichrist (first beast) be obeyed and worshipped.

Few Christians realize just how close the revealing of the antichrist is. This is because Christ words and warnings about the end-of-this-age are ignored in most pulpits. Most of God's people have stopped up their ears from hearing important Biblical end-of-this-age truth.

This damning cancellation of Christ's words and God's promises of the coming millennial reign of Christ is explained by the Apostle Peter: *"Knowing this first of all, that scoffers will come in the last days with scoffing, following their own sinful desires. They will say, "Where is the promise of his coming? For ever since the fathers fell asleep, all things are continuing as they were from the beginning of creation."* (2 Peter 3:3-4).

In addition, the Apostle Paul warns: *"For the time is coming when people will not endure sound teaching, but having itching ears they will accumulate for themselves teachers to suit their own passions, and will turn away from listening to the truth and wander off into myths. As for you, always be sober-minded, endure suffering, do the work of an evangelist, fulfill your ministry"* (2 Timothy 4:3-5).

## Powers of Darkness Removing Obstacles

As god of this world, Satan has tried many times to set up a one-man world ruler. The Apostle John explains: *"Children, it is the last hour, and as you have heard that antichrist is coming, so now many antichrists have come"* (1 John 2:18).

Hitler was a recent modern antichrist who attempted to dominate the whole world. In recent times, other antichrist type leaders have cropped up, only to fall short of global dominance, affecting only a few countries and some regions.

The forces of righteousness, the free democracies of the world, and the Holy Spirit's work of convicting of sin, judgment, and righteousness have been able to halt these satanic attempts of ruling the world. In the end, which is soon, Satan will be allowed to put a premier maniacal dictator in control of the whole world.

The slow removal of the forces of righteousness is allowing the powers of darkness to advance Satan's deceitful plans. Part of Satan's plan is to create worldwide chaos by weakening true democratic nations, especially America. All to create a perfect storm of lawlessness along with global political and economic instability.

Peoples of the world are being programmed and manipulated into near hysteria, yearning for a leader to fix all these terrible problems and restore peace and tranquility.

The Apostle Paul prophetically points to this very hour where the mystery of lawlessness works to set up the final antichrist for complete global control: *"For the mystery of lawlessness is already at work. Only he who now restrains it will do so until he is out of the way. And then the lawless one will be revealed, whom the Lord Jesus will kill with the breath of his mouth and bring to nothing by the appearance of his coming. <u>The coming of the lawless one is by the activity of Satan with all power and false signs and wonders</u>, and with all wicked deception for those who are perishing, because they refused to love the truth and so be saved"* (2 Thessalonians 2:7-10).

## The Wicked Given Over to a Delusion

Progressively, evil is called good, and good is called evil in most cultures worldwide, especially in America.

Yes, America leads the way in sexual perversion, corruption, violence, crime, and greed. Every righteous pillar in America has been weakened, dismantled, or removed. The last restraints against wickedness and lawlessness are being broken down as the wicked attack law and order—attempting to upend equal justice, basic freedoms and replace local police forces with a national law enforcement system[2].

Hatred of law and order, fueled by bitter jealousy and greed, as well as universal obsession with sinful pleasures has finally moved God to send a strong delusion upon the wicked. Many in America and the world have rejected conscience to the point of no return.

---

[2] **Example of a National Police Force from History:** Hitler's Brown Shirt Henchmen called The Sturmabteilung (SA) literally meaning "Storm Detachment", was the Nazi Party's original paramilitary wing. These thugs were trained for the primary purposes in providing protection for Nazi rallies and assemblies; disrupting the meetings of opposing parties; fighting against the paramilitary units of the opposing parties. When Hitler took over Germany, secret law enforcement grew nationally, known as the SS and became the racial policy of Nazi Germany and general policing, whereas the Waffen-SS consisted of combat units within Nazi Germany's military. A third component of the SS was the "Death's Head Units", this police force ran the concentration camps and extermination camps. [Excerpt from Wikipedia online Encyclopedia]

*"Therefore God sends them a strong delusion, so that they may believe what is false, in order that all may be condemned who did not believe the truth but had pleasure in unrighteousness"* (2 Thessalonians 2:11-12).

## Also, Wholesale Christian Deception

Christianity, as the last bulwark against satanic deception and immorality has also become victim to Satan's work of corruption. As light and salt to the world, God's people have fallen into what Christ said would happen when God's people fall in love with the world and live for the cares of this life: *"You are the salt of the earth, but if salt has lost its taste, how shall its saltiness be restored? It is <u>no longer good for anything except to be thrown out and trampled under people's feet</u>"* (Matthew 5:13).

How did the bulk of Christianity lose its way? Jesus explains what happens as the end-of-this-age comes to its final years: *"See that no one leads you astray. For many will come in my name, saying, 'I am the Christ,' and they will lead many astray"* (Matthew 24:4-5).

Many false teachers have come on the scene over the last seventy years captivating masses to follow their teachings. Most of these teachers basically state that those who embrace their teaching will become Christlike Christians.

Unfortunately, these teachers learned how to mimic the Christian walk by formulating their own version of what a Christian's walk looks like. They developed a special "how to" teaching that encourages their followers to copy their special formula.

These false teachers become intermediaries, misleading Christians away from personally knowing and obeying the true Christ—in essence they cause deceived Christians to follow them, instead of Christ.

Thus, the false teach in Christ's name but offer a different Jesus, just as the Apostle Paul described: *"I am afraid that as the serpent deceived Eve by his cunning, your thoughts will be led astray from a sincere and pure devotion to Christ. For if someone comes and proclaims another Jesus than the one we proclaimed, or if you receive a different spirit from the one you received, or if you accept a different gospel from the one you accepted, you put up with it readily enough"* (2 Corinthians 11:3-4).

The Apostle Paul labeled these types of false Christian leaders as deceivers: *"For such men are false apostles, deceitful workmen, disguising themselves as apostles of Christ. And no wonder, for even Satan disguises himself as an angel of light. So it is no surprise if his servants, also, disguise themselves as servants of righteousness. Their end will correspond to their deeds"* (2 Corinthians 11:13-15).

The Apostle Peter also gave this dire warning: *"But false prophets also arose among the people, just as there will be false teachers among you, who will secretly bring in destructive heresies, even denying the Master who bought them, bringing upon themselves swift destruction. And many will follow their sensuality, and because of them the way of truth will be blasphemed. And in <u>their greed they will exploit you with false words</u>"* (2 Peter 2:1-3).

## Prosperity and the Love of This Age

America has been blessed with prosperity. However, that prosperity made way for a major false teaching to grip the hearts of most Christians. Known as the prosperity message, false teachers made the following words of Christ into a demonic trap: *"The thief comes only to steal and kill and destroy. I came that they may have life and have it abundantly"* (John 10:10).

**The abundant life syndrome:** Many popular teachers were unwilling to research the correct translation of the word "life" in this passage, mistaking the word life to mean life for Christians on Earth should be abundantly prosperous. A horde of false teachers turned this verse in the Gospel of John into a cottage industry to make money. Many popular ministers and ministries have become personally wealthy, running multimillion-dollar ministries of greed.

They took the word "life" to mean that the blessings on Earth should be in abundance; money, happiness, wealth, health, and in some false teachings, this life in the world as a Christian should be luxurious.

Twisting and turning certain Scripture out of context, these false teachers convinced their massive following that by giving to their ministry, they would reap material, financial, and health rewards. *In their greed they will exploit you with false words.*[3]

The true meaning in this passage for the word "life" comes from the Greek word, "zōē" which means: The life we receive from Father God through Christ his Son, is to be abundant. The main aspect of God's abundant life is described by the Apostle Paul as the fruit of God's presence within our life: *"Love, joy, peace, patience, kindness, goodness, faithfulness, gentleness, self-control"* (Galatians 5:22-23).

## Asleep at the Darkest Hour

Jesus warned that most end-of-this-age Christians would be asleep and not realize the end-time signs pointing to Christ's soon return are in full swing. *"As the bridegroom was delayed, they all became drowsy and slept"* (Matthew 25:5), and warned: *"So also, when you see these things taking place, you know that he is near, at the very gates"* (Mark 13:29).

False doctrine, the love of the pleasures in this life and the cares of this life have become a deadly trap for most believers. *"But watch yourselves lest your hearts be weighed down with dissipation and drunkenness and cares of this life, and that day come upon you suddenly like a trap. For it will come upon all who dwell on the face of the whole earth. But stay awake at all times, praying that you may have strength to escape all these things that are going to take place, and to stand before the Son of Man"* (Luke 21:34-36).

Few Christians are awake and ready to endure the end-time troubles that are now coming upon America and the world in full force. Most Christians are spellbound and blinded by false teachings they have learned to embrace. In a drunken like stupor, they cling to what America was and are stuck in denial of Christ's end-time warnings. Few Christians dare to embrace

---

[3] **Pat Robertson's Law of Reciprocity:** This is one example of the many last days greedy ministry teachings, which is a scheme to manipulate followers to give generously to Robertson's ministry, by twisting Christ words; *"Give, and it will be given to you"* (Luke 6:38). This boils down to being a money raising scheme that motivates followers to give money to get more money and other blessings in return, which is just plain greed.

Christ's harder words that produce true Christlike character to become prepared to endure to the end of this age.

## The Mystery of Lawlessness

The suppression of truth, as well as free speech, the cancellation of an unbiased-free press, and the limiting of self-protection and economic freedom has suddenly come upon America. A mysterious spell began to grow in the American culture, allowing corrupt people in business and politics to lie and cheat their way into power. With one harmonizing theme, "Globalism" where the sovereignty of free nations is to be eliminated to foster a "no-border" world.

I believe the mystery of lawlessness that the Apostle Paul saw has finally come to its fruition. Lawlessness has quickly gained power to control and manipulate the masses through fear and criminal use of political power, legal power, and law enforcement. Blatant bitter hatred and rebellion have become political weapons, as behind-the-scenes powers of darkness enlist anarchists to incite riots to get their way and tear down opposition.

All voices of opposition, conservatism, and righteousness have died off, become marginalized or criminalized—in one way or another—they have or are in the process of being cancelled.

The summer of 2020 riots were protests led by anarchists and bankrolled by multi-billionaires. These acts of lawlessness, in conjunction with the insidious way that Covid-19 virus invaded America and the world, mysteriously helped usher in complete political upheaval in the November elections.

Political and legal lawlessness has grown rapidly with little opposition. The very fabric of American freedoms, backed by law and order is disintegrating and being replaced by despotic policing on a national level, attempting to nullify local and state law enforcement.

## Political and Spiritual Leadership Vacuum

This political and social upheaval, along with America's weak Christian leadership, (who moaned and groaned about all that is taking place, while ignoring Christianity's lukewarm condition) placed leaders in power who are void of courage and righteousness.

As the birth pains of the physical coming of the kingdom of God increase, along with divine judgments on a national and global basis, political and spiritual chaos is about to explode.

The outlook for the masses will be full of gloom and doom, just as Christ warned: *"And there will be signs in sun and moon and stars, and on the earth distress of nations in perplexity because of the roaring of the sea and the waves, people fainting with fear and with foreboding of what is coming on the world. For the powers of the heavens will be shaken"* (Luke 21:25-26).

Already the Biden administration is overwhelmed by gas shortages, the border crisis, Mideast turmoil, and wild inflation due to foolish spending to buy votes, which keeps corrupt politicians in power.

**Are the signs that we are seeing** in the sun, moon, and stars that Jesus spoke of include Navy pilot reporting strange flying objects in the sky?

### The Devil Knows His Time Is Short

Yes, the powers of heaven are being shaken and underneath this invisible upheaval, the earth is reeling. Satan knows his time is short and he will soon be cast out of heaven: *"Now war arose in heaven, Michael and his angels fighting against the dragon. And the dragon and his angels fought back, but he was defeated, and there was no longer any place for them in heaven. And the great dragon was thrown down, that ancient serpent, who is called the devil and Satan, the deceiver of the whole world—he was thrown down to the earth, and his angels were thrown down with him"* (Revelation 12:7-9).

> "THEREFORE REJOICE, YOU HEAVENS AND YOU WHO DWELL IN THEM! BUT WOE TO THE EARTH AND THE SEA, BECAUSE THE DEVIL HAS GONE DOWN TO YOU! HE IS FILLED WITH FURY, BECAUSE HE KNOWS THAT HIS TIME IS SHORT."
> REVELATION 12:12

Satan has an end-time battle plan, even though he knows he will lose in the end. In rage he will bring great trouble upon the Earth and attempt to bring an end to true Christianity and destroy Israel as a nation.

## Setting Up for the Antichrist Rule

Satan is determined to glorify himself in opposition to our heavenly Father's will by planting evil people throughout the world. Jesus said of Satan, when Satan influenced Peter to oppose God's will concerning Christ's own death: *"But he turned and said to Peter, "Get behind me, Satan! You are a hindrance to me. For you are not setting your mind on the things of God, but on the things of man."* (Matthew 16:23).

Now, as the end-of-this-age unfolds, the devil will use evil people that he has groomed and amassed as his human minions, to help set up the antichrist rule. Jesus explained this in the parable of the Weeds in Matthew 13:36-43.

We see political leaders and mega business owners lean towards communism and encouraging the breakdown of moral norms among the nations and throughout America—to gain political and economic control. Satan's "seeds of weeds" have grown to maturity, where years of subtle conditioning of the masses has paid off.

All the idolatrous love, of the pleasures of this life, has helped groom the masses and a multitude of weak, unprepared, lukewarm Christians to look for a savior who will promise prosperity and peace. A leader who will take control of the chaos and lawlessness and bring the world back to order and stability.

## The Man of Lawlessness Will Captivate the Masses

God is allowing the world to be shaken to its very core when Satan is finally cast out of heaven. There has been a progressive increase in lawlessness, chaos, and persecution towards Christians and Israel, as the devil manipulates the masses to clamor for a human-political savior to arise on a worldwide level.

Therefore, Scripture refers to the antichrist as the man of lawlessness. The antichrist works within Satan's plan of creating fear and instability to usher in a human savior, who promises calm and stability, to captivate the idolatrous loyalty of the masses.

How will Satan elevate a mere human to godlike stature and force him to be worshipped and obeyed? The answer is not of this world.

## Was God an Astronaut?
*Exponential Progression of Idolatry of Ancient Aliens*

In 1968, Erich von Däniken published the blockbuster book, "Chariots of the Gods," with the subtitle "Was God an Astronaut?" This volume was pivotal in boosting the mythical idea that certain pieces of archaeological history and strange unexplainable recorded historical encounters were signs of extraterrestrial beings visiting Earth.

Most theologians overlook the phenomenal rise in this belief that has gripped the masses and even captivated many Christians—the belief that extraterrestrial life does exist. Over the last 100 years the idea of life on other planets or within another universe has gained a solid hold on the minds and hearts of the masses.

Movies, books, eyewitness accounts of UFOs, abductions by alien life, and scientific search to contact E.T. have grown exponentially[4]. The military and other government agencies have

---

[4] **Exponential:** Extremely rapid increase in the belief that beings from another world exist who are to be feared, held in awe, and honored. This phenomenon began slowly, however there were key pivotal influences that have propelled the notion of Extraterrestrial Life in leaps and bounds, such as science fiction literature and movies.

tracked many of these encounters yet continued to suggest that they are all explainable.

However, recently the US Navy has finally released actual video recordings of unexplained UFO sightings by their pilots.

Now a much-anticipated report of these secret encounters will be released in June of 2021. John Ratcliffe, the top intelligence official under former President Donald Trump, explains what's in the forthcoming report, "a lot more sightings than have been made public. Some of those have been declassified."

In a recent Foxnews.com report dated May 15, 2021, concerning the soon to be released UFO report, Luis Elizondo, a former defense official who spent years investigating unidentified aerial phenomena told the network program that the vehicles have technology vastly exceeding any human invention. "Imagine a technology that can do 600 to 700 G-forces, that can fly 13,000 miles an hour, that, that can evade radar and can fly through air and water and possibly space, and oh, by the way, has no obvious signs of propulsion, no wings, no control surfaces and yet still can defy the natural effects of Earth's gravity. That's precisely what we're seeing," Elizondo states.

### A Neurotic Obsession With E.T. Beings

In 1938 the Mercury Theatre presented a radio broadcast in a "breaking-news" format, reporting on the radio that a real invasion by Martians was taking place.

Orson Welles presented this news-like program with an occasional disclaimer throughout the broadcast.

Announcements that this was only a play—not a real happening—did little to squelch the public hysteria that spread nation-wide. The graphic details of fake destruction and the hideous descriptions of the aliens and their machines filled the minds of the listeners with horror and fear. This was another pivotal jolt to the increased belief in extraterrestrials throughout the American culture.

Mass production of science fiction movies and literature is constantly distributed to satisfy the obsessive intrigue of the existence of E.T.. Through the fifties right up to now, books, films, documentaries, conspiracy theories and block buster movies captivate multitudes who take in these sci-fi works to be most likely true. An ET neurosis has invaded the unconscious minds of most people worldwide, especially in America.

The 1951 sci-fi movie, "The Day the Earth Stood Still" was another pivotal cultural mind bender. This thrilling movie portrayed a humanoid alien coming to America in a flying saucer

to warn the world of its imminent doom and destruction if the use of nuclear weapons was not stopped.

In this portrayal, a robot with terrible powers enforced fear upon the whole world. The aliens (in human form) had developed a race of robots, empowered to act as a police force and having unlimited god-like power and authority to destroy people, civilizations, or a whole planet. Any planet who rebelled against this so called enforced unified peace would automatically be eliminated.

To terrify the Earth and all its nations to submit to this new planetary system of peace and order, the alien and its robot caused everything on Earth to stop operating for one half hour, with exception of medical emergencies and airplanes in flight.

The alien is pursued and killed by the military police. However, the alien's robot takes the dead alien's body back to their flying saucer and brings him back to life. (A not-so subtle inference to the antichrist and the second beast, exercising power to make great signs and make fire come down from heaven in front of people, where the antichrist suffers a mortal wound and then comes back to life.)

These science fiction myths continue to program the whole world's sub-conscious and create fearful expectations that aliens exist and are more advanced than mankind.

The Star Wars movies and books, along with the Star Trek franchise have created cult followings. Movies like Superman, 2001: A Space Odyssey, E.T. the Extra-Terrestrial, War of the Worlds, Alien, Cocoon, Close Encounters of the Third Kind, Contact, Signs, and countless other movies[5], keep feeding and growing a collective fear and trepidation as well as a surreal expectation that sooner rather than later, the Earth will be formally visited by extraterrestrial beings. They will come either to conquer, enslave, destroy, or help the Earth solve its many problems.

An organization called Search for Extraterrestrial Intelligence (SETI) offers software that can be downloaded from the Internet on home computers to help with more computing power to analyzes radio telescope data.

E.T. and alien images are very common now. What was once considered in the not-so-distant past to be hideous demonic beasts are now thought of as extraterrestrial intelligent life forms that can possibly help the world overcome its many problems.

The movie E.T. helped children of all ages and adults accept the existence of life from outer space as friendly, superior in power, and more intelligent than humans—despite that the E.T. character looked grotesque and non-human.

---

[5] A list of more than 1,200 movies depicting extraterrestrial life can be found on the Internet website Wikipedia. This list does not include Television shows or TV series depicting aliens from another world visiting Earth (TV shows such as My Favorite Martian, The Invaders, and Mork and Mindy).

Most fifties kids idolized the TV series "Superman" that portrayed an alien in human form who was cast upon the Earth as an infant. This extraterrestrial grew up and appeared as a man with supernatural powers and became a savior and avenger against evil in episode after episode.

## Supernatural Powers, Sorcery — Saturating America

Parallel to the rise of the belief in other world aliens, there is phenomenal interest in human inner spiritual powers. Spiritualism and sorcery have become another spell binding interest indirectly tied to the possibility of aliens who have supernatural powers.

A big boost in the belief in human supernatural powers came with the 1986 release of Shirly McClain's book titled "Out on a Limb" that espoused new age spiritualism, the practice of astral projection[6], relating these spiritual activities to the mystery of UFOs.

This and other books such as the Harry Potter series help expand the interest in delving into human supernatural powers that basically amount to the practice of sorcery.

Scripture forbids the practice of sorcery for a very profound reason—the effect of sorcery is real, powerful, and produces harmful results. The power of darkness orchestrated by Satan is to enthrall as many people as possible to seek supernatural powers, teaching how to awaken the dormant powers of the human spirit.

Even in Christianity, false teachings have led believers to practice sorcery by learning to pray selfishly and wrongly. False spiritual gifts are common in many denominations and fellowships.

As a pastor, I have engaged in many battles forced upon me or on others in our fellowship by wayward Christians praying wrongly.

One incident took place years ago where a group of Catholic Christian parents were in the grandstands praying for their high school football team to win.

I was an assistant volunteer coach on the opposing team and noticed how sluggish our team was performing. Our team had a

---

[6] **Astral Projection:** The ability to project one's personal spirit to leave one's body temporarily and travel. Though not scientifically proven, many have testified to this kind of experience that can influence other people spiritually and physically.

good record for the year; however, the boys were making dumb mistakes against a team that had to this point a mediocre season.

Looking out across the field I noticed the parents of the opposing team mouthing prayers with great intensity. It was then that I realized these good Catholic parents were practicing sorcery. They were praying that our kids would not do their best, causing our team to make mistakes and not execute plays on a level they normally performed.

From years of dealing with these kinds of carnal prayers that are not of God and are harmful, I immediately prayed silently that these curses be broken. I prayed that the best team win. Within two or three plays later our team came to life and by the end of the game our team came out on top—easily.

The powers of sorcery and witchcraft are now a common activity throughout our culture. It is a widespread story that Tom Brady's wife, Gisele Bundchen practices incantations and mantras to aid Brady's team and his success as a quarterback. Any form of sorcery is evil!

Now, I often refer to this generation as the "Harry Potter generation" because of the widespread practice of sorcery, mystic new age practices, and the increased growth in Wiccan[7] and other cult and occult movements.

Another cult formed by Ron L. Hubbard started in the 1950's. This cult is based on the beliefs and practices performed by extraterrestrial beings dating back 70 million years. Hubbard's teachings are summarized in a book he published entitled, "Dianetics: *The Modern Science of Mental Health"*

Scientology is now considered a UFO religion in which the existence of extraterrestrial entities operating unidentified flying objects (UFOs) are an element of belief within Scientology.

Many famous people live by these teachings which are managed and disseminated by a religious organization called the

---

[7]**Wiccan** or Wicca is a neo-pagan (meaning "new pagan") religion that was created by a British man named Gerald Gardner in the mid-to-late 1940s. Gardner popularized the new religion through books he published in 1949, 1954, and 1959. They are entitled High Magic's Aid, Witchcraft Today, and The Meaning of Witchcraft. Gardner called Wicca the "witch cult" and "witchcraft" and called its followers the Wicca or simply "the craft".

Church of Scientology. You may recognize some of the names who embrace Scientology: Kirstie Alley, Anne Archer, Tom Cruise, John Travolta, and Greta Van Susteren to name a few.

Many people suffer from past trauma and defilements from a life of sin or were raised in an abusive or dysfunctional family. Because of this, the desire to become spiritually empowered to internally experience good mental health and emotional stability is widespread. Cult teachings like Dianetics within Scientology provide methods to spiritually suppress these past stains and wounds.

Furthermore, many Evangelical, Charismatic, and Pentecostal Christians have become hungry for spiritual power apart from the harder teachings of Christ and God's healing grace and discipline, in God's timing.

The gifts of the Holy Spirit are real and are to be sought after with the right motives of heart. The gifts are dispensed by the Holy Spirit and: *"Are empowered by one and the same Spirit, who apportions to each one individually as he wills"* (1 Corinthians 12:11). They are not downloaded on demand by power craving carnal Christians who want to be known as having the power of God, like Simon the magician, as recorded in the book of Acts. (See Acts 8:14-21.)

One must be disciplined in dying to inner selfish motives for seeking a spiritual gift. Believers by the masses seek the power of God in the form of a spiritual gift or a so-called "Holy Spirit manifestation" to expunge bad thoughts and ill feelings.

These deceived Christians are tricked into taking a short cut, only to temporarily suppress the internal issues of their heart and personal spirit. These lingering hidden issues are stains on one's inner being from past trauma or defilements and produce uncomfortable thoughts and feelings.

Unfortunately, few embrace God's training program and discipline in becoming qualified to receive a gift of the Holy Spirit. Rather most Charismatic Christians lust after the power of God and fall victim to satanic counterfeit gifts.

Many become obsessed with signs and wonders and lust after false spiritual manifestations. The bizarre antics witnessed by outsiders of such exotic manifestations often refer to these activities as insane, just as the Apostle Paul warned: *"If, therefore, the whole* *church comes together and all speak in tongues, and outsiders or unbelievers enter, will they not say that you are <u>out of your minds</u>?"* (1 Corinthians 14:23).

## Signs and Wonders Syndrome
*Believers Spellbound by False Signs and Wonders*

Adding to end-time signs Christ warned about is the increase in false signs and wonders. When the antichrist is finally revealed and moves into global domination, Christ warned that deception by false christs and false prophets would become vexing: *"For false christs and false prophets will arise and perform great signs and wonders, so as to lead astray, if possible, even the elect"* (Matthew 24:24).

Christians are being prepped by false spiritual manifestations that will condition many believers to fall for the devil's last days deception performed by the second beast of Revelation: *"And by the signs that it is allowed to work in the presence of the beast it <u>deceives those who dwell on earth</u>, telling them to make an image for the beast that was wounded by the sword and yet lived"* (Revelation 13:14).

## Christians Duped by the E.T. Myth

In November 2009, the Vatican hosted a five-day conference of scientists from around the world to study the possibility of alien life. Funes, a Jesuit priest, helped coordinate the conference. As a Vatican representative on this research he said, "How can we rule out that life may have developed elsewhere? Just as there is a multitude of creatures on Earth, there could be other beings, even intelligent ones, created by God. This does not contradict our faith, because we cannot put limits on God's creative freedom."

Many Protestant Christians believe the same thing and a multitude of Christians have enjoyed Hollywood's entertaining alien movies as already mentioned.

 In chapter 22 of his 1960 book "My Answer" Billy Graham answered the question about life on other planets, Graham was asked:

"I am a student of the physical sciences. Some of my associates are inclined to believe that there is life on other planets. If there are people who inhabit these planets, what does that do to our faith in the Gospel? Can it be that God is primarily interested in this planet?" [Graham's answer:]

"From my studies in the Scriptures, I can find nothing that would change our essential faith in the Gospel if we did discover life on other planets. Our Bible is clearly designed for this particular planet with its particular problem of man's sin. When we observe this fact we are on safe ground. It is not a part of the Bible's message to inform us of what God has done elsewhere. Its message is concerned with earth dwellers, their origin, the reason of their existence, the cause of their misery and the plan of redemption for a fallen race. I am sure that if there are dwellers on other planets, they are either not involved in the sin problem, or else God has made satisfactory provision for them. The God of the Universe is the God of our Lord Jesus Christ. He is entirely able to support the entire creation and is able to govern it in righteousness."

Over the years Billy Graham answered this question many times with basically the same answer:
- Life in outer space is not mentioned in Scripture and life beyond the Earth was not part of the Bible's message.
- Nothing about the discovery of extraterrestrial life would undermine any essential element of the Christian faith—Billy Graham personally believed that extraterrestrial life exists.
- Though he initially allowed for the possibility that God had made satisfactory provision for fallen aliens, eventually he decided that only mankind was fallen in the universe, therefore, aliens did not need salvation, and only mankind was the special focus of the universe.

In a recent Charisma Online article written by Dayton Maxwell covering the US government's report to be released in June 2021 on UFO sightings he suggests the following:

A report that concludes even the possibility of extraterrestrial visitation will definitely be profound. This would mean that life exists on other planets, and they are superior to us, at least in their technology.

This raises several questions to those of us who are Christians:
- Did God create life on other planets as He did on Earth? Do these aliens share the same values we are taught by Jesus?
- What is the possibility that these aliens are responsible for all communications written in the Bible that we attribute to God, including the birth and life of Jesus?
- Is what we consider supernatural totally understood by aliens with their advanced technology, and nothing is supernatural to them?
- No prophet in the Bible has written about life outside of Earth. Prophecies have been accurate about events that come about on Earth, so why has God not revealed to earthly prophets the existence of life elsewhere?
- Has God revealed to some living today who, like the prophets of old, could inform us of life elsewhere and how we should interact with them?
- The Bible contains predictions of events yet to come, particularly in the book of Revelation. The indications are that severe natural disasters are a part of these events. Will aliens with a significantly advanced knowledge intervene to help in some manner, or could they even be causing such disasters?
- Satan exists. What might aliens know about Satan and how he operates on Earth? Does Satan exist elsewhere also to confound their lives?
- Why have these aliens not communicated with us? Has God instructed them not to communicate with us, like He doesn't permit communications between us and those in heaven (with rare exceptions)? Should we seek communications with them?

Also, another article by Dayton Maxwell posted on Charisma Online, entitled "For Response to Coming Government UFO Report, We Need Modern-Day Einstein, Isaiah" Maxell writes:

> "A U.S. government report on Unidentified Flying Objects (UFOs) is expected to be "profound and transformational" in content. If it concludes that we are likely being visited by aliens from other worlds but they have not contacted us, much remains unknown. Speculation will be rampant. What is the level of

technology of these aliens? Why don't they contact us? How do they transport themselves through space? Is our God also their God? If they choose to contact us, could they provide technology that could solve all our earthly problems, make us healthier to live much longer and generally make our lives much more satisfying? Or will nothing change because they fully intend to leave us totally alone?... Yet one story in the Bible could be described as UFO travel. The prophet Elijah was taken to heaven while still alive by a chariot (2 Kings 2:11-12). Was that a UFO? On the other hand, there is nothing in the Bible about beings like us living on other planets. It only talks about heaven, heavenly beings and the Holy City of Jerusalem being prepared to be put on Earth (Rev. 21). We need a prophet like Isaiah to tell us about beings on other planets, their relationship to God, how we may eventually communicate with them as part of God's universe, and what we can expect if we get to know them."

These Christian opinions are not an exception but rather a representative mindset of millions upon millions of believers. (A massive number of Christians are unbelievably gullible and ignorant of Scripture and are at risk of taking the mark of the beast.)

### A Fallen Angel Emerges From the Nether Gloom
*Disguised as an Extraterrestrial Enforcer of Good*

The truth is that the existence of extraterrestrial beings and the supposed images of extraterrestrial aliens are satanically inspired caricatures of demons or fallen angels. Billions of people of all nations, including millions upon millions of Christians gaze at these hideous images, unknowingly and indirectly worshiping demons. Like stooges, multitudes are being subtly programmed to accept the rise of the second beast disguised as an extraterrestrial being and follow its orders and worship the antichrist!

The possibility of Satan deceiving the whole world, including multitudes of Christians, by a fallen angel physically appearing as an extraterrestrial life form with great power and superior intelligence is not farfetched—it fits in Scripture.

Indeed, Apostle John, if he viewed one of the modern-day movies loaded with images of an E.T., he would certainly describe it as a demonic entity or a fallen angel.

## Does Scripture Clarify the Existence of Ancient Aliens?

Yes, in the form of fallen angels! In Jude it states, *"And the angels that did not keep their own position but left their proper dwelling have been kept by him in eternal chains in the nether gloom until the judgment of the great day"* (Jude 1:6).

A third of the angels rebelled, siding with Lucifer and left their proper dwellings in the heavens. God judged them to hell (nether gloom) only to allow them in the last days to emerge and deceive the wicked, letting Satan set up his rule on earth.

As true believers, we are to understand all the schemes of Satan so we may not be caught off guard. Having the second "Beast" of Revelation appear as a brilliant and powerful extraterrestrial, coming to earth to help, is a Biblical explanation and a most plausible end-of-the-age scenario.

**Just a reminder about angels of God visiting Earth in the past:** We find the following Biblical account that clears up any confusion: *"When man began to multiply on the face of the land and daughters were born to them, the sons of God saw that the daughters of man were attractive. And they took as their wives any they chose. Then the LORD said, 'My Spirit shall not abide in man forever, for he is flesh: his days shall be 120 years.' The Nephilim were on the earth in those days, and also afterward, when the sons of God came in to the daughters of man and they bore children to them. These were the mighty men who were of old, the men of renown.* (Genesis 6:1-4). God pulled the plug on the sons of God (angels) fooling around His human creation.

Reading Revelation and the Apostle John's description of the four living creatures and the twenty-four elders around God's thrown, one might think they are watching a scene from Star Wars. *"Then I looked, and I heard around the throne and the living creatures and the elders the voice of many angels, numbering myriads of myriads and thousands of thousands, saying with a loud voice, 'Worthy is the Lamb who was slain, to receive power and wealth and wisdom and might and honor and glory and blessing!'"* (Revelation 5:11-12).

A third of the myriads and thousands upon thousands of these angels went AWOL and followed Lucifer in rebellion. These angelic beings are at war with the angels of God and Christ

(Lamb of God) in an end-of-this-age fight over control of the Earth and all of God's human creation. These angelic beings existed eons before God created Adam and Eve in His own image. The angels exposed themselves to God's human creation from time to time, and are now in rebellion.

## Fallen Angels and Demons Lose Invisibility

When finally kicked out of heaven, Satan, his fallen angels, and his minions (a multitude of demons) have only the Earth on which to perform their last moments of rebellion and destruction.

*"And I heard a loud voice in heaven, saying, 'Now the salvation and the power and the kingdom of our God and the authority of his Christ have come, for the accuser of our brothers has been thrown down, who accuses them day and night before our God. And they have conquered him by the blood of the Lamb and by the word of their testimony, for they loved not their lives even unto death. Therefore, rejoice, O heavens and you who dwell in them! But woe to you, O earth and sea, for the devil has come down to you in great wrath, because he knows that his time is short!"* (Revelation 12:10-12).

Satan's plan to deceive the whole Earth's population has been in the making for some time. If he loses the battle for heaven and is thrown down to earth as Scripture declares, he will have developed a perfect cover to deceive most of the peoples on Earth.

This plan of Satan's has been in the making for thousands of years—a gradual and methodical progression of strange being manifestations to set the stage for the grand lie: that the bad angels and demons are merely extraterrestrials coming to help.

## Conspiracy Theory or Bible Prophesy Unfolding

As the end-of-this-age nears all the trouble Christ warned about will increase in frequency and intensity. Fear, panic, and uncontrolled hysteria will cause rumors and conspiracy theories to spread like wildfire throughout the populations of the whole world.

Christians who play church, making themselves unprepared to endure the coming troubles, because they ignored Christ's warning words about the end, will rush about looking for help and end up embracing the mark of the beast. Just as Christ warned in the parable of the Ten Virgins, they will lose their salvation and be left behind:

*"Then the kingdom of heaven will be like ten virgins who took their lamps and went to meet the bridegroom. Five of them were foolish, and five were wise. For when the foolish took their lamps, they took no oil with them, but the wise took flasks of oil with their lamps. As the bridegroom was delayed, they all became drowsy and slept. But at midnight there was a cry, 'Here is the bridegroom! Come out to meet him.' Then all those virgins rose and trimmed their lamps. And the foolish said to the wise, 'Give us some of your oil, for our lamps are going out.' But the wise answered, saying, 'Since there will not be enough for us and for you, go rather to the dealers and buy for yourselves.' <u>And while they were going to buy, the bridegroom came</u>, and those who were ready went in with him to the marriage feast, and the door was shut. Afterward the other virgins came also, saying, 'Lord, lord, open to us.' But he answered, 'Truly, I say to you, I do not know you.' Watch therefore, for you know neither the day nor the hour"* (Matthew 25:1-13).

The foolish Christian will wake up to all the trouble and realize the return of Christ is at hand, but they will listen to all manner of conspiracies, false news, and false prophesies just as Christ warned: *"Then if anyone says to you, 'Look, here is the Christ!' or 'There he is!' do not believe it. For false christs and false prophets will arise and perform great signs and wonders, so as to lead astray, if possible, even the elect. See, I have told you beforehand. So, if they say to you, 'Look, he is in the wilderness,' do not go out. If they say, 'Look, he is in the inner rooms,' do not believe it. For as the lightning comes from the east and shines as far as the west, so will be the coming of the Son of Man"* (Matthew 24:23-27).

Even now many Christians are seeing the handwriting on the wall and freaking out. In their unprepared state, they fear what is coming upon the world, just as Christ warned: *"People fainting with fear and with foreboding of what is coming on the world. For the powers of the heavens will be shaken"* (Luke 21:26).

They will panic like unbelievers over their income, investments, retirement, food, belongings, toilet paper and gas shortages, and their loss of a passive life of ease. Like God's people in Isaiah's day, they fear what man and what end-times troubles can do to them: *"For the LORD spoke thus to me with his strong hand upon me, and warned me not to walk in the way of this people, saying: "Do not call conspiracy all that this people calls conspiracy, and do not fear what they fear, nor be in dread. But the LORD of hosts, him you shall honor as holy. Let him be your fear, and let him be your dread. And he will become a sanctuary and a stone of offense and a rock of stumbling to both houses of Israel, <u>a trap and a snare</u> to the inhabitants of Jerusalem"* (Isaiah 8:11-14).

Christ warned Christians to stay awake and not let the cares of this life become a trap: "*But watch yourselves lest your hearts be weighed down with dissipation and drunkenness and cares of this life, <u>and that day come upon you suddenly like a trap</u>. For it will come upon all who dwell on the face of the whole earth. But stay awake at all times, praying that you may have strength to escape all these things that are going to take place, and to stand before the Son of Man"* (Luke 21:34-36).

The true conspiracy is the fact that Satan has been working behind the scenes, using fallen angels, demons, and his evil human minions to facilitate his last days takeover of the world. God has allowed all this to demonstrate to the world His word of truth.

In his vision the Apostle John saw Christ coming on a white horse and: *"He is clothed in a robe dipped in blood, and the name by which he is called is <u>The Word of God</u>"* (Revelation 19:13).

### Signs, Fire, Fear—Forcing Antichrist Worship

The masses of the world, frightened and weary of all the troubles, will gaze in amazement while watching news broadcasts of strange signs and false prophetic words performed by the second beast of Revelation.

Years of conditioning from movie/TV depictions of alien powers will cause millions upon millions to become breathless and fall for the great signs that this fallen angel performs (posing as an extraterrestrial creature).

Many lukewarm and unprepared Christians will be mesmerized by the second beast's power as it causes fire to come out of the sky in front of people.

Most people will step in line and humbly and fearfully obey and make images of the antichrist. Faced with the threat of death, even skeptics will fall in line.

During the COVID 19 panic, people were herded into obedience with social distancing, masks, and isolation by incomplete scientific research. Jesus warned about the last days pandemics, earthquakes, natural disasters, energy shortages and economic instability, to the point of: *"And there will be signs in sun and moon and stars, and on the earth distress of nations in perplexity because of the roaring of the sea and the waves, people fainting with fear and with foreboding of what is coming on the world. For the powers of the heavens will be shaken"* (Luke 21:25-26).

The stage is being progressively set to easily coerce multitudes into submitting to faulty science and technology schemes to manage the world's population on every level of living.

### Ending Lawlessness, Restoring Control and Order
*A Despotic Lockdown of Freedoms for the Common Good*

The antichrist and second beast's system will be enforced—to save the world's population from global economic collapse and famine; where inflation, corruption, crime, lawlessness and anarchy, drug and human trafficking cartels, and a tax-free underground economy will be eliminated:

> Where a global universally mandated system of accountability is established to maintain social order and to track and control such things as pandemic vaccinations, all buying and selling transactions, monitor and control travel

and international migration, all to be implemented and managed with available technology.

Where the sovereignty of all nations and individual freedom must become subjected to an authoritarian system of rules and regulations that will be beneficial for all the peoples of the world.

A system that is fair, free from political corruption, and free from special interest influence that cannot be hacked or hijacked and is immune to any data processing attacks.

The rule and management of this system must be put in the hands of a trusted leader accepted by the world's majority population—where opponents are relegated to complete silence—preventing any renegade groups from undermining global community harmony.

This global rulership must have authority and power to suppress any form of rebellion, crime syndication, or the formation of any underground secret societies.

This system must have the artificial intelligence capacity and ability to detect and predict an individual's social proclivities and the ability to intervene and suppress wrong thinking or bad attitudes before bad behavior is reached. All this to be based on everyone's individual data profile and facial recognition through artificial intelligence monitoring, eavesdropping, invasion of privacy, spying, and profiling.

Far-fetched? Then consider China's social credit initiative:

> This "˜system calls for the establishments [sic] of unified record system for individuals, businesses, and the government to be tracked and evaluated for trustworthiness. Initial reports suggested that the system utilized numerical score as the reward and punishment mechanism; recent reports suggest there are in fact multiple, different forms of the social credit system being experimented with. Numerical system has been implemented only in several regional pilot programs, while the nationwide regulatory method has been based primarily on blacklisting and whitelisting. The credit system is closely related to China's mass surveillance systems such as Skynet, which incorporates facial recognition system, big data analysis technology, AI (Artificial Intelligence) and Project Maven (Artificial Intelligence Arms Race)." [Quotation from Wikipedia Free Online Encyclopedia, Social Credit System Article.]

The world is racing towards a perfect set of difficulties, distresses, and unsolvable perplexities—where natural disasters, economic collapse, and humanitarian calamities (such as pandemics, famine, and uncontrolled immigration), as well as lawlessness (crime and violence)—demand that a real new-world-order become reality.

## And Now, America Is Morphing Into a Socialistic Hybrid

For years it has been difficult to imagine America, land of the free and home of the brave, could ever face losing its constitutional freedoms. But now Satan's human minions boosted by the powers of darkness, have inched their way into every American institution.

Their goal is to transform our independent republic of unified individuals into a socialistic hybrid culture, a mixture of socialism, communism, and capitalism, driven by an oligarchy[8] and all disguised as democracy. Government and corporate America have merged, where leadership is facilitated by a handful of billionaire elites and political opportunists.

Americans have enjoyed many features of a democratic government, such as elections and freedom of speech; however, those freedoms are being suppressed without any voted-in referendum. Now, powerful corporations ran by affluent individuals have greater say and control in making political policy, far more than the ordinary citizen.

Oligarch elitists control a biased news media, most social media platforms, communication, Internet database structures, and information distribution.

These elitists operate in the shadows, financially supporting politicians and decision makers who advocate for a socialistic approach in the governance of America's society and culture.

These affluent individuals have a significantly larger influence on policymaking than ordinary citizens. This is a form of corporate communism that keeps the ordinary citizen dependent on the elite and a legislation of rules and regulations that favor the affluent.

---

[8] Oligarchy: a small group of people having control of a country, organization, or institution. Modern countries ruled by oligarchy politics are Russia, China, Saudi Arabia, Iran, Turkey, South Africa, North Korea, Venezuela. The United States is considered by many to be a mixture of a democratic government controlled by a class of "elite powerful" with their influence hidden from public scrutiny.

Almost overnight by sleight of hand, the United States jumped in leaps and bounds towards a purer hybrid of a socialistic, communistic, and capitalist rule. Where capitalistic oligarchists practice communistic suppression of free speech, religion, and free enterprise.

Much of the American populace passively embraced this sleight of hand transformation. They have been blinded by the cares of this life, a high level of prosperity, and distracted through spellbinding entertainment and lust for luxury living.

There are millions upon millions of Americans who oppose this change of political and social ideology but are silenced. They are cancelled through political pressure, or have become content with the status quo, too busy struggling at making a living to become a political influence for righteous change.

The powers of darkness and Satan's last days' scheme will take a giant swath of these freedom loving people and compel them to happily comply. Many will fall in line as the world falls apart and then suddenly beholds the revealing of the antichrist and his plan to straighten everything out.

## The Antichrist, a God Chosen by the Gods
*Hand Picked by the Second Beast of Revelation*

Satan must contend with all those freedom loving citizens of the world, especially in America. Though most people will long for a savvy leader to straighten the mess out, the task will be perceived as way above the intelligence and ability of any known leader. Because of inept world leadership, not just anyone can fill this position and satisfy the majority. Satan's man of the hour must appear to be exceptional, superhuman, and able to pull off miracles.

Speaking of this person, Scripture says of him: *"One of its heads seemed to have a mortal wound, but its mortal wound was healed, and the whole earth marveled as they followed the beast. And they worshiped the dragon, for he had given his authority to the beast, and they worshiped the beast, saying, "Who is like the beast, and who can fight against it?"* (Revelation 13:3-4).

Granted, this description of the antichrist (first beast of Revelation) is loaded with symbolism. However, the basic message is that the antichrist will be empowered by Satan and be raised to life, mimicking the true Christ's death and resurrection.

To seal the deception for as many human beings as possible, even the bulk of Christianity, God will allow Satan to make one of his fallen angels emerge from the nether gloom. This fallen angel will appear as a god-like extraterrestrial with prophetic powers—the second beast of Revelation.

It will command allegiance with great signs and even make fire come down from the heavens. But the allegiance he commands will be directed towards the antichrist: *"Then I saw another beast rising out of the earth. It had two horns like a lamb and it spoke like a dragon. It exercises all the authority of the first beast in its presence, and makes the earth and its inhabitants worship the first beast, whose mortal wound was healed. It performs great signs, even making fire come down from heaven to earth in front of people, and by the signs that it is allowed to work in the presence of the beast it deceives those who dwell on earth, telling them to make an image for the beast that was wounded by the sword and yet lived"* (Revelation 13:11-14).

Thus, Satan uses a fallen angel disguised as an extraterrestrial with god-like power to deceive and convince the world that the antichrist, though human, is a god to be worshipped and obeyed.

## True Christianity and Israel in the Way

God has always had a remnant of Christian believers hiding out during dark times, especially at the end-of-this-age. Through the centuries, true Christianity can be accredited with many advances in peoples and cultures of the world, where many turned to God and sought righteousness.

It is the true believer in Christ who is deeply hated by Satan. In Revelation chapter 17, Scripture speaks of a false Christianity that makes a deal with the antichrist, but in the end is betrayed by the antichrist. Many theologians believe that the apostate Protestant denominations become aligned with the Church of Rome (The Catholic Church) to form this end-time harlot church.

It is the true Christian and the fellowship of the saints that Satan makes war against. We see persecution against true Christianity on the rise worldwide, including America.

Jesus said that the true and final move of God would come through a people of God who have been refined by intense persecution. In Matthew 24 Christ explains what happens to the last days true Christian: *"Then they will deliver you up to tribulation and put you to death, and you will be hated by all nations for my name's sake. And then many will fall away and betray one another and hate one another. And many false prophets will arise and lead many astray. And because lawlessness will be increased, the love of many will grow cold. But the one who endures to the end will be saved. And this gospel of the kingdom will be proclaimed throughout the whole world as a testimony to all nations, and then the end will come"* (Matthew 24:9-14).

Notice in this passage Christ describes what message will be proclaimed by those Christians who endure this coming hate filled trouble directed at true believers. It is the gospel (good news) of the coming kingdom of God—not to a few, but to every nation throughout the world.

Just as Satan has a plan to deceive the whole world, God has a plan to bring forth the truth of Christ's soon-to-come physical reign on Earth. This proclamation will ignite Satan's wrath even more and push for the antichrist to be revealed and exalted.

At this point hostility between Israel and the various factions of the Palestinians and other Muslim nations will become a "monkey-wrench" in the antichrist's promise of global peace. Thus, Israel must be convinced that the antichrist (not Christ) is Israel's long-awaited savior. Israel will allow the antichrist to declare himself as god in the Jewish most holy place: *"So when you see the abomination of desolation spoken of by the prophet Daniel, standing in the holy place (let the reader understand)"* (Matthew 24:15).

When this event takes place, all hell will break lose throughout the world, which will be the start of the Great Tribulation. The terrible trouble that ensues will accelerate the need for a global system to track, manage, and ensure lives are safe, saved, food is properly delivered, vaccines are administered effectively, and all opposition is headed off at the pass, preventing rebellion, anarchy, and sabotage.

# Sci-Fi Becomes Reality
*Integrating Science, Technology and Behavioral Sciences*

Jules Verne is considered the father of science fiction. With noted books such as: Five Weeks in a Balloon (1863), Journey to the Center of the Earth (1864), From the Earth to the Moon (1865), Twenty Thousand Leagues Under the Seas (1869-70), Around the Moon (1870).

These and other writings by Jules Verne as well as other early Sci-Fi authors stretched the imagination of children and adults around the world. They were fiction based on futuristic scientific achievement.

Now consider the modern fusion of science, technology, Information Technology, Mobile Transaction Technology, and Behavioral Sciences.

Indeed, man has set foot on the moon and continues to explore outer space, inner space (psychology – sociology - medicine), and the depths of the ocean. We control environmental comfort, monitor home security, execute money management, and other conveniences with ease.

The advent of technical tools such as semi-conductor micro-chips, wrist phones, cell phones, and data processing, I.T. server farms and cloud I.T. services were in the not-so-distant past considered science fiction.

People can travel locally or around the world with ease and speed. Yet war, potential nuclear holocaust, hate, crime, sickness, the harmful elements of the Earth (quakes, storms, drought), radiation from the sun, and falling outer space objects (asteroids) cannot be managed. The Earth's population is one cataclysmic event away from being severely reduced in size or even destroyed.

The prophet Daniel speaks of the time that we are in now. This prophet of God saw God's people and the nation of Israel in the Great Tribulation, where people would scurry about the world and knowledge would increase: *"At that time shall arise Michael, the great prince who has charge of your people. And there shall be a time of trouble, such as never has been since there was a nation till that time. But at that time your people shall be delivered, everyone whose name shall be found written in the book. And many of those who sleep in the dust of the earth shall awake, some to everlasting life, and some to shame and everlasting contempt. And those who are wise shall shine like the brightness of the sky above; and those who turn many to righteousness, like the stars forever and ever. But you, Daniel, shut up the words and seal the book, until the time of the end. <u>Many shall run to and fro, and knowledge shall increase</u>"* (Daniel 12:1-4).

And very soon, the fictional representations of Sci-Fi aliens from other planets visiting the earth will become a reality. Fallen angels and demons will be kicked out of heaven and come to Earth in rage and revenge. They will manifest gradually. Leading the way will most likely be the appearance of the second beast of revelation then later in waves of tormenting beings (demons) from the bottomless pit during the wrath of God.

But first, how will Satan, through his two henchmen (the beasts of Revelation), deceive the world to buy into Satan's plan for paradise on Earth?

### Utopia: The Cloud, 666 Science, and Fear of Death

To manipulate and coerce the world into his counterfeit utopia, Satan must first bring the world into chaos, lawlessness, and tribulation. But Satan's plan leads into God's wrath and dystopia[9].

We see the world edging towards tyrannic rule by the few, where democracies become ruled by the wicked, not led by the righteous. America was never designed to be a pure democracy, but a democratic republic using checks and balances to prevent mob rule, where most of its citizens are swayed to elect rulers (not leaders) who have greed and special interest at heart—putting at great risk equal rights and fairness towards all its citizens.

Satan has navigated around these checks and balances in most democracies and especially in America through prosperity and passivity, undermining morality and setting the stage for the breakdown of law and order.

Technology and consumer convenience, along with misinformation are deceiving the masses and herding them towards Satan's new world order. Millions are passively embracing the ease of buying and selling without handling money, as well as many other instant-digital amenities.

Amazon and other major online retail services along with powerful cloud computing and transaction processing systems have become a giant steppingstone for Satan's end time plan to bring his version of utopia to the world.

---

[9] **Dystopia and utopia:** Dystopia is defined as a fictional community or society that is undesirable or frightening. Utopia is an imaginary community or society that possesses highly desirable or nearly perfect qualities for its citizens.

Once the Great Tribulation begins, when the antichrist is revealed, expect the appearance of the second beast disguised as an E.T. alien to solve all the world's problems by forcing its 666 mark in the form of a human microchip.[10]

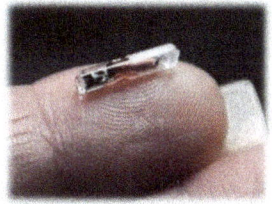

As the world currencies become inflated and worthless, and a cashless system becomes necessary. Then medical information and individual identification must be infallible for travel, entering dining facilities, or a government building. Then the cloud, the Internet, and instant verifiable personal identification for all transactions must become a global law enacted for survival and global common good. Anyone refusing faces death!

**Humanity is being digitally transformed into slavery, conditioned to be totally dependent on the system of the coming antichrist rule and control.**

## The Great Tribulation and the Final Harvests

When the antichrist is revealed to the world, Christ warns of the following: *"For then there will be great tribulation, such as has not been from the beginning of the world until now, no, and never will be. And if those days had not been cut short, no human being would be saved. But for the sake of the elect those days will be cut short"* (Matthew 24:21-22).

God, in his faithfulness will give the world and all the nations a choice. Either turn to the true Christ, hold out for the rapture and the physical return of Christ, or follow the antichrist and take the mark of the beast.

---

[10] **A human microchip** implanted by making a mark or incision just underneath the skin and then inserting an electronic device. Examples include an identifying integrated circuit RFID device encased in silicate glass which is used to implant the device in the body of human beings. This type of subdermal implant usually contains a unique ID number that can be linked to information contained in an external database, such as personal identification, law enforcement, medical history, medications, allergies, and contact information. Now Quantum Dot technology is advancing, using transdermal patches to label people with invisible ink to store medical and other information subcutaneously (beneath the skin).

Multitudes will come to Christ wholeheartedly; this is the harvest of the righteous and the rescue of true Christians commonly known as the rapture. *"Immediately after the tribulation of those days the sun will be darkened, and the moon will not give its light, and the stars will fall from heaven, and the powers of the heavens will be shaken. Then will appear in heaven the sign of the Son of Man, and then all the tribes of the earth will mourn, and they will see the Son of Man coming on the clouds of heaven with power and great glory. And he will send out his angels with a loud trumpet call, and they will gather his elect from the four winds, from one end of heaven to the other"* (Matthew 24:29-31).

From the Apostle John's Revelation, we read of this future event: *"After this I looked, and behold, a great multitude that no one could number, from every nation, from all tribes and peoples and languages, standing before the throne and before the Lamb, clothed in white robes, with palm branches in their hands, and crying out with a loud voice, "Salvation belongs to our God who sits on the throne, and to the Lamb!"* (Revelation 7:9-10).

In John's vision, it was explained that this multitude are: *"These are the ones coming out of the great tribulation. They have washed their robes and made them white in the blood of the Lamb"* (Revelation 7:14).

As for the wicked left behind: *"So the angel swung his sickle across the earth and gathered the grape harvest of the earth and threw it into the great winepress of the wrath of God"* (Revelation 14:19).

The true Christian who is prepared to leave this world and not look back will be raptured by God's angels. They will have to endure the Great Tribulation for a season *"But for the sake of the elect those days will be cut short."* However, the rapture takes place before the wrath of God falls upon the world. *"For God has not destined us for wrath, but to obtain salvation through our Lord Jesus Christ, who died for us so that whether we are awake or asleep we might live with him. Therefore encourage one another and build one another up, just as you are doing"* (1 Thessalonians 5:9-11).

And the Apostle Paul also states: *"Behold! I tell you a mystery. We shall not all sleep, but we shall all be changed, in a moment, in the twinkling of an eye, at the last trumpet. For the trumpet will* sound, and the dead will be raised imperishable, and we shall be changed" (1 Corinthians 15:51-52).

By the way, when the rapture occurs those left behind will wail in travail and all of Israel will realize that the antichrist was a lie, that Christ was indeed their savior, the one they rejected and crucified: *"Behold, he is coming with the clouds, and every eye will see him, <u>even those who pierced him</u>, and all tribes of the earth will wail on account of him. Even so. Amen"* (Revelation 1:7).

## After the Rapture, God's Wrath and Christ's Return

The book of Revelation describes just how terrible the coming wrath of God will be as it befalls those upon the Earth after the rapture of the saints. Just as God parted the Red Sea to rescue Israel from the army of the Pharoah, so to the sky will part and open up like a scroll: *"When he opened the sixth seal, I looked, and behold, there was a great earthquake, and the sun became black as sackcloth, the full moon became like blood, and the stars of the sky fell to the earth as the fig tree sheds its winter fruit when shaken by a gale. The sky vanished like a scroll that is being rolled up, and every mountain and island was removed from its place. Then the kings of the earth and the great ones and the generals and the rich and the powerful, and everyone, slave and free, hid themselves in the caves and among the rocks of the mountains, calling to the mountains and rocks, "Fall on us and hide us from the face of him who is seated on the throne, and from the wrath of the Lamb, for the great day of their wrath has come, and who can stand?"* (Revelation 6:12-17).

One of the first acts of destruction will be huge meteor showers pelting Earth. There will be plagues, extreme scorching heat from the sun, and a horde of locusts (demons) released from the bottomless pit that will torment people night and day: *"They were allowed to torment them for five months, but not to kill them, and their torment was like the torment of a scorpion when it stings someone. And in those days people will seek death and will not find it. They will long to die, but death will flee from them"* (Revelation 9:5-6).

Since most of the people left in the world continue to worship demons, thinking they are aliens from another planet, God will release demons perceived by the masses as extraterrestrial beings: *"In appearance the locusts were like horses prepared for battle: on their heads were what looked like crowns of gold; their faces were like human faces, their hair like women's hair, and their teeth like lions' teeth; they had breastplates like breastplates of iron, and the noise of their wings was like the noise of many chariots with horses rushing into battle. They have tails and stings like scorpions, and their power to hurt people for five months is in their tails. They have as king over them the angel of the bottomless pit. His name in Hebrew is Abaddon, and in Greek he is called Apollyon"* (Revelation 9:7-11).

I can go on with more horrifying descriptive Scripture of the coming wrath of God in detail, but it is better that you study Revelation and other end-time Scripture for yourself.

In the bowls of wrath and plagues there is an amazing reality: *"The rest of mankind, who were not killed by these plagues, did not repent of the works of their hands nor give up worshiping demons and idols of gold and silver and bronze and stone and wood, which cannot see or hear or walk, nor did they repent of their murders or their sorceries or their sexual immorality or their thefts"* (Revelation 9:20-21).

Instead, *"People gnawed their tongues in anguish and cursed the God of heaven for their pain and sores. They did not repent of their deeds"* (Revelation 16:10-11).

**Finally, Christ returns physically** to set up the kingdom of God on Earth to reign for a thousand years: *"And I saw the beast and the kings of the earth with their armies gathered to make war against him who was sitting on the horse and against his army. And the beast was captured, and with it the false prophet who in its presence had done the signs by which he deceived those who had received the mark of the beast and those who worshiped its image. These two were thrown alive into the lake of fire that burns with sulfur. And the rest were slain by the sword that came from the mouth of him who was sitting on the horse, and all the birds were gorged with their flesh"* (Revelation 19:19-21)

He will return with the saints who had died and those raptured and rule the nations with an iron rod: *"And the armies of heaven, arrayed in fine linen, white and pure, were following him on white* horses. From his mouth comes a sharp sword with which to strike down the nations, and he will rule them with a rod of iron. He will tread the winepress of the fury of the wrath of God the Almighty. On his robe and on his thigh he has a name written, King of kings and Lord of lords" (Revelation 19:14-16).

Again, I suggest that you read in Revelation how the end turns out and how at the end of the millennial reign of Christ on Earth this happens: *"Then I saw a new heaven and a new earth, for the first heaven and the first earth had passed away, and the sea was no more. And I saw the holy city, new Jerusalem, coming down out of heaven from God, prepared as a bride adorned for her husband. And I heard a loud voice from the throne saying, 'Behold, the dwelling place of God is with man. He will dwell with them, and they will be his people, and God himself will be with them as their God. He will wipe away every tear from their eyes, and death shall be no more, neither shall there be mourning, nor crying, nor pain anymore, for the former things have passed away.'"* (Revelation 21:1-4).

## Knowing the Truth Does Not Make One Ready!

Jesus warned his disciples (and us) about the times that we are in now—the end-of-this-age: *"And there will be signs in sun and moon and stars, and on the earth distress of nations in perplexity because of the roaring of the sea and the waves, people fainting with fear and with foreboding of what is coming on the world. For the powers of the heavens will be shaken. And then they will see the Son of Man coming in a cloud with power and great glory. Now when these things begin to take place, straighten up and raise your heads, because your redemption is drawing near"* (Luke 21:25-28).

In addition, he warned: *"But watch yourselves lest your hearts be weighed down with dissipation and drunkenness and cares of this life, and that day come upon you suddenly like a trap. For it will come upon all who dwell on the face of the whole earth. But stay awake at all times, praying that you may have strength to escape all these things that are going to take place, and to stand before the Son of Man"* (Luke 21:34-36).

Many who read these words of Christ and believe that time has come are still not ready. That knowledge alone will not prepare one to be able to endure the coming persecution and the difficult times during the Great Tribulation. Rather, we who believe must act on our beliefs and follow all of Christ words. The need to prepare and how to prepare is simply put by Christ with this parable: *"Everyone then who hears these words of mine and does them will be like a wise man who built his house on the rock. And the rain fell, and the floods came, and the winds blew and beat on that house, but it did not fall, because it had been founded on the rock. And everyone who hears these words of mine and does not do them will be like a foolish man who built his house on the sand. And the rain fell, and the floods came, and the winds blew and beat against that house, and it fell, and great was the fall of it"* (Matthew 7:24-27).

Do not cherry pick your favorite Scriptures of promise and ignore the harder words of Christ. Work with leaders who expound on Scripture properly, who see and warn about what is now upon America and the world. Listen to pastors and teachers who lead by example, point to the lordship of Christ, and know what it means to die to the old carnal nature.

Many leaders today are enemies of the work of the cross within the believer's life. When we all stand before the judgment seat of Christ, we have no excuse of falling short of Christ's commands—we cannot blame our pastor because each of us know how to read Scripture for ourselves and seek the true Christ.

The Apostle Paul writes: *"In him we live and move and have our being'; "'For we are indeed his offspring.' Being then God's offspring, we ought not to think that the divine being is like gold or silver or stone, an image formed by the art and imagination of man. The times of ignorance God overlooked, but now he commands all people everywhere to repent, because he has fixed a day on which he will judge the world in righteousness by a man whom he has appointed; and of this he has given assurance to all by raising him from the dead."* (Acts 17:28-31).

And that day is right around the corner. Satan will come upon the world in great wrath to steal away as many as possible.

You know now that the appearance of the second beast of Revelation will most likely come disguised as an extraterrestrial being to deceive, if possible, even the elect.

*"For false christs and false prophets will arise and perform signs and wonders, to lead astray, if possible, the elect. But be on guard; I have told you all things beforehand."* Mark 13:22-23

## Contact Information

You can contact the author by the following:

**Mail:**  MC Global Ministries
 Charles Pretlow
PO Box 857
Canon City, CO 81215
**Phone:** (719) 285-8542
**Email:** contact@mcgmin.com

Charles is available as a guest speaker. His extensive background in ministry, counseling, and end-of-this-age issues provides sound instruction on overcoming the last-days troubles and wounds to the personal spirit and damaged emotions.

### More About the Author

Pastor Charles Pretlow is one of the founders of MC Global Ministries and Wilderness Voice Publishing. Charles began his ministerial work in 1974 and shares insights gained from years of study, ministry, and counseling Christians who struggled in their walk with Christ. He shares sound teachings to help equip the sincere Christian and those in leadership to effectively minister in these dark days leading to Christ's return. Charles' theology is practical, founded in years of experience and training in the discipline of the Lord.

www.ingramcontent.com/pod-product-compliance
Lightning Source LLC
Chambersburg PA
CBHW060458050426
42451CB00009B/706